Mario Petrucci

Moonbird : love poems

Fair Acre Press

First published in Great Britain on 14th February 2023
by Fair Acre Press
www.fairacrepress.co.uk

A CIP catalogue record for this book is available from the British
Library.

ISBN   978-1-911048-74-9

Cover image: author's adaptation of an online (public domain)
photograph (2020).

Acknowledgements

Moonbird, *We Nameless* and *Ship* draw loosely on the following Rumi poems (respectively): 'IX. Every moment the voice of Love...'; 'XVII. I was on that day when the Names...'; 'XVIII. Before thee the soul is hourly...'. *Selected Poems from the Divani Shamsi Tabriz*, tr. R.A. Nicholson (Kitab Bhavan, New Delhi, 2014), was the source text.

the kiss and *We Nameless* were published in *Acumen* 100. *Moonbird* appeared in *Poetry & All That Jazz 2021*.

*

Future editors should note that the concreteness many of these poems display is best recaptured using the typeface in which they were originally composed: Times New Roman. Moreover, any idiosyncrasies in these texts (such as repetition of, and variable capitalisation across, titles; or extra vertical space between stanzas) are very much intentional.

CONTENTS

here is the deepest secret nobody knows...
the wonder that's keeping the stars apart

E. E. Cummings

for Jo

who breathes these poems with me

Moonbird

From every compass-point of self: Beloved, I hear You.
Through momentary partings of cloud, I glimpse a blue
beyond distraction. You too are of heaven: we each bear
the goosebumps of angelic quills. Flight: our truest nation.

But love flies us further than morning, higher than angels:
when bodies, their seeded lands of dust, succumb to currents
of purity. We fell – but have a way up, each of us a wing
for the eagle that leads its camel, dumb yet noble with sand.

Your sea-scent reaches me on that breeze beyond breezes.
Dawn brings its once rent moon: separate halves rising, merging,
making whole. You are air sprung of water: so these hooves dare
to make Your cloud-shoal a home. Look closer: see our twin

pearls accrued from one oyster. Return us to union, for even
an ocean of weeping is pure. Sea thunders, heavy as ointment;
sky rolls its furrows – but there is light here, the sure light that
wakens. Is this at last our joint flight, our unsleeping tomorrow?

few

have ever arrived as you
do – so live
your tender palm on my

small of back – warmer
than skin on skin
closer

kin of lackless order
nearer than blood
an aroma

taken fully in
through bone & heart
born together

in that first black
flash – that
lone-love of Cosmos

in initial rush
unmerging Its fire &
water just so

we might later relearn
this hush
so yearned in the other :

a sweet re-making
that slakes our sun whose
flow becomes many

whose few – me with
you &
only you – burns

as One

We Nameless

In sleep I returned to that dawn before Names:
before woman, man, nor material thing, carried
the same. Named and Name stumbled far apart
as lovers caught either side of steepest sierra or
fraught sea. There was neither 'I' nor 'We'. I
asked of God in advance: one strand of Your hair
to lead me back, to lance this maze of lives. No:
the skies gazed their blueness as still as Your eyes
tender with morning. I stormed all religion from
Islam to Christ. Each Cross and Kaaba: vacated.
I trekked worlds for temple, stupa, pagoda: nothing
sated. Not even loss. I ascended Moses' highest
mountain, drew within smack of heaven. There
was no Sistine finger.
          At last I lingered in this
teeming red ark of my chest – heard Your rain
here: softer forms of God whose kiss melts me.
You and I: one nameless Name. You are Me,
I You, in that heartmost heart. Nowhere else.

what a kiss can Do

how always we consider lips
yet there is what slips between words
what is unearthed between breaths as much
as that soft shift in supple muscle behind liquid folds:
supple wound found as birthing cleft of hips

which is the world bereft
of love kissing itself by whatever means:
each larva pushed into gaping yellow of chick or sun
perfectly subsumed by beloved disc of moon
or the cliff-side flushing forth its clear
raked rush of monsoon

which is how I near you
hushed with Self – lava to lava –
south to north – steady with risk – hollow
with spilled – lying upon you or beneath you in
loving eclipse ready to be emptied by you
which is utterly to be filled

for one kiss
fluttering this rift of Love
alters all – is that pebble dropped
in the cosmic pool that ripples to flicker
the greening blade at its shore that brings
the blackly started stallion back
to drink and swells the fish
alive with spawn

So think of this
when dawn with dusk strives
across night to brush lips: that when
space relents and finally we embrace drawing
tight with faces close enough to taste each sating mutual
musk of skin: that when these eternally unbending ages come
to what must surely be an end so our dust-made bodies
along their trembled lengths at long pure last may
kiss: we consummate everything
there is with everything
there is

few

words
now will do – as lone bird to
sky or

cosmos
to such eyes as yours whose blue
speaks

word
-lessness to depths as at my touch
breath

molten
from your sweet-flowing breast
drowns

oceans

when

I find the petals in me
you are opening that blossoms me

or sun's molten metal
you are emptiness gently to carry me

when I fill my moon
you are that silveriness to spill me

no longer alone
you are love that marries me

So – whenever you wish
whatever you wish

let me be ocean's rim
that comes to you

seas that miss yet
never fish you

these waters
you swim that

moment
to moment

kiss you

Virus

Held within distance
is means for intimacy more

bracing than embrace or
in absence so individually felt

more presence than kisses:
have nations seen how isolation

melts into touch that is
touchless... something precious

no longer rationed
a flinging to love almost

too much?
What is this breath

breathed so
separate as togetherness

so that even
if Death should dare

for each
each may reach

there as Us?

the kiss

let this kiss
we share be more than ours alone

for each longing
hour must kiss the day in which it belongs

as rains with abandon
flush most-barren dust to raise earth's green yeast

and yes: strangers who walk
proper and apart sublimely touch with heartfelt glance

so love will raise our dead
as if life were that least linen bed we at last climb into

for flocks feast on dark
swarms whose soft offspring bless the carcass bird

so yes: let these self
-same lips brush in a place beyond sky-rinsed

skies or murdering
clocks and let that holy Face we each in

Love resemble
purse desiring lips as we do now to

defeat space
and time – as fire in the flame

repeats to
make so many of the few

Ship

You freed my soul to slip as fast grains do – through
their neck of hourglass. So it is, I grow as I diminish.
How may lips reach You? This needy tongue of sand?

Wherever You step – a pulse beats up, flush with earth.
How to wash hands of You, that fragrance of rain on dust?
Even apart, so pent with distance, I know Your smell.

If Your moon leaves these skies of brain, skull's firmament
wanes with mourning, hair's night-cloud liverish with lament.
To make room for You, I unfurnish eyes, cells: vanish for Your

love of nothingness. For one tropical kiss, all temperance flames.
This body: a hull, so still in pursuit of You, my named harbour.
Without metre, footless, I skim Your dark swells of water.

Moon : Bird : Sea

Your breasts: silvered shoals of moonlit foam. I
dock a head-dark egg there – Neptune's queendom.

Those shallows in Your chest ripple their underwater
bars of bone. You are ocean's plume – whatever it is

in high-flown moons that returns a gaze. That ark of
rays splayed behind You: a peacock's albino on pitch.

Your hand sly-sliding where no one touches is water
swelling water: I spill white sand between Your long

thighs, such wide quills of sweet alabaster. Rising
over our sheet's night-strand, Your eye is a tide

of looking – Your desire a moon taking flight
to overtop my sea walls. We make of brack

pale crops of fire, our earnest calls cliff to
cliff swoop us back, feathered rocks that fall

once more, again, to our wrack nest. Our *Yes*
half-sung asks: what are we for, if not to bring

impossibles to union, finding bird in ocean, moon
in bird? So Love: crack me as moon does its sea-shell,

dwell in one flesh as the egg in horizon's curve. Take
me – break with a kiss these flightless shores, kind tsunami.

&

how
much is our I-with-We
(
this Us-in-You each one becomes
)
no verb noun or seething thing-some part of
speech
but in-betweens of life's conjunctions / punctuations
those
!!!!!! love brings to aftermath rooting silence as saplings
do
grassland or our many ,,,,,,, slowing tongues' sweet brahmas
or
each : of button reached in seeming darkness You undo where
—
rushed as much as near-withheld becomes bodies' plug-in
touch
flushes to scissoring legs' acetylene-weld ; then this
((
which is our spooning double-parenthesis in
praise
of beds whose open-ended aside spills
wide
days in whom nights never quite
end
.
yet most of all feel
these thrilling ands and and-
hands that weave our co-making Eve-
Adam dust keeps apart though leaping 1 heart
no   may we never un-read this Love we have into

treatise or book but keep those little bridges ridging
the palate-top mouth into breath-stopping sigh
for who'd wish for high love looked up in
death or its dictionary when stars fan
to their darks between [yes even
worlds of words are sand to
this unwhispered please
to our beheavened
once-more
kiss of
&

Your hands : these

hands wan as night doves
entwining feathers – twin birds fretting
to find a perch among hastening lips, brows, waists…

this is how we reach for midnight brightness that flares
with dark: we two lain alongside – jostling beds
as if vying to hatch our planetary

egg of love. Undressed You
slip wet, are air-boned glass: my taste that
preens You, this fast tongue that fills You, yet no eyes see

what fingertips do: Your hair's vineyard where doves rest
-lessly brood among moonlit tendrils until
at last four-winged hands

roost pace-cascading breath as
this nest they bring themselves to between
Your breasts. Tonight we are that Bird deathless within

the bird, Flight beyond flight, each wordless kiss that
sings us to eloquent being. Love: how
are we ever apart if nightly

even alone You dream me? And while these
hearts so moonless are locked together
sleeping how can we know

throughout these silent rooms with all
their many hands
whether the clocks are moving?

that Curvature

love is
whose sun comes to
rise because night entire turns
for light's burning water – or how a planet

endures itself past swerved horizons revealed
breach on breach though only to one
who will step towards what
cannot be reached

and so I
see how small how
fleet a world is forever falling
away from every point one enters it – and yet

love I step ever roamless toward you knowing
your fall towards me undressed no less
mysterious as what loves
redress

as if this
brief togetherness
of dawn (even our parting
kiss) were blessed as a woman liquid with

love turning to her lover in sleep : or is it
this palm flat to your bare flats
of belly my hand spread
there so steady

that seems a young husband darkened
by labour dawdling down to that
mown swell of field your
body makes home?

diver

across the net
I watch you sleeping
in this live benthic rinse of screen

that bed a wreck of green fluorescence
you lie lead-heavy so
static

yet
something in you flies
underwater as those birds who make of tide

skies
– deep and
deeper you have learned to breathe water

and though fate leaves us bodies apart
through you our skin becomes
same ocean

as looking down for you in nervous
light I feel so slight this
wakeful boat I'm

in: between us
that sag and tug of line
and one electric swerve of current

what stone remembers

waking in pitch to
sense alongside that length of another
boned with night &

dense with love –
blind flesh stitched together by touch at
many points as though

two tectonic tongues
had rediscovered themselves across aeons
to grind wet heat where

they meet turned from
jointedness to flow so slow so stealthed
in darkness – for when

what was sundered in hardness at last
finds itself deeply un-
wronged as souls burning in pairs

unspurned by grieving
first sleepy with kisses then
barely breathing

world
can be whole again

coda

moon lit

there is sun in you

as ready heats
within their yellow star
will swirl themselves among
themselves to complete that smile
startled to your surface

or as the photon
enmeshed in in-lit plasma your soft
-seared cry
circulates unceasing within you
a million years wise before
final release

for when one body lies
upon another in near-consummation
this is peace in secret eclipse
where dimness dares
to flare with Now-ness the pagan
ages bow to

So I
make of myself sky
either may refuse in which
you freely move
whose eyes meet mine
unseen in unseeing
darkness &
choose

Ingram Content Group UK Ltd.
Milton Keynes UK
UKHW050144300323
419362UK00011B/195

9 781911 048749